Roy and Phyllis on their wedding day, Portsmouth 1936

Westfield Mill, Ossett, Yorkshire

BASIC TRAINING 1940
ROYAL SIGNALS
YORKSHIRE

The Love Letters of
Pte. Roy Barton

Printed edition 2022
Publisher: Hillfort Books, England
hillfortbooks@gmail.com

Introduction

The Second World War saw the sudden expansion of army regiments and to meet these new demands the Royal Corps of Signals established a Basic Training centre for new recruits at Westfield Mill near the small mill town of Ossett, Wakefield, Yorkshire.

In November 1940, with his younger brother George having already been called-up and undertaken his Royal Signals training in Whitby, Roy Barton too received his call-up papers while working in the family fancy-goods store in Portsmouth. He arrived at the Signal's training depot at Westfield Mill and in the following five weeks of Basic Training, Roy wrote 23 letters in 35 days to his young wife Phyllis whom he had left behind in Glastonbury, Somerset. In them he described in detail life at Westfield Mill, the challenges and demands of each day, the characters of his fellow conscripts, his feelings of separation from his wife, the friendliness of the Yorkshire people and ultimately, he questions his suitability to become an officer.

Roy's letters and his accompanying scrapbook of photos and documents from those days are a record of the military and the social life of those extraordinary times and are unique in the records of any British regiment in World War Two.

Following his Basic Training, Roy trained as a wireless operator in Huddersfield before, in 1942, joining the Royal Signals section of the GHQ Liaison Regiment (known as Phantom) attached to General Montgomery's HQ Main based at Richmond, Surrey. In August 1944, Roy crossed the Channel and in the following 15 months wrote to Phyllis over 200 more letters of great detail as he travelled with Monty's HQ through Northern Europe into Germany.

Those letters, along with this Basic Training group, are all published by Hillfort Books under the title;

'DEAREST PHYL...'
Letters of Love and War 1940-45.

Basic Training - Royal Signals
Westfield Mill, Ossett, Yorkshire
November 1940 - January 1941

On Tuesday the 21st of November 1944, while stationed in Belgium, Roy wrote to Phyllis remembering his first day in the Army four years earlier and how their separation on his conscription in 1940 had initially affected him.

My Darling Wife,

Four years ago this morning, November 21st 1940, we left 34 Wells Road just before 7.00am. My heart and spirits were just about as low as they possibly could be. After taking the bus to Wells we stood on the station for the Bristol train. Never in my life did I long so much for the non-arrival of a train, bus, boat or what have you. It was a cheerless morning I know – winter had crept in early that year; snow had already fallen in the north and the prospect for the future in the south was not milder by any means. The prospect for my own personal future was even darker. I was to join the army.*

The sight of the train seemed just like the end of life itself. Nobody could venture the day I would see you again; by the feeling inside me it might have been never at all. That morning my dearest, you seemed more precious to me than at any time during the twelve previous years I have known you. You were more to me than life itself, on this earth and all succeeding lives put together. Even as you lay in my arms the night before, soft, warm, infinitely desirable, more precious than all the riches the world could gather, the perfect lover, wife and companion, the dismal future before me and the horror of the morning was so heavy upon me that I could no more have possessed you than leaped out of the upstairs window. It was like the sentence of death.

     I remember that feeling as the train pulled out and you were left on the station, and how I cursed that bridge which put you so quickly out of sight. That horrible feeling of loneliness and sadness stayed with me until I caught first sight of you on Leeds station two months afterwards. That feeling, dearest love, is with me today and I will have it with me every moment until I see you again.
I love you so much.
With all devotion,
Roy
**Glastonbury*

The following letters from Roy's Basic Training camp, were written to Phyl at her father and stepmother's home in Glastonbury, Somerset.

Pte RWS Barton 2356364
Squad 282,
'D' Company,
3rd Signals Training Company,
Ossett,
Yorkshire

Saturday 23rd November 1940
Dearest,

Here sits your husband in the YMCA canteen, a fully-fledged soldier complete in battledress, gaiters and forage cap. The din in here is terrific. Tobacco smoke fills the air and the noises of voices, piano and the clatter of plates makes it about impossible to concentrate.

Today we had an issue of kit which just about made me the biggest chap in the British Army! We had our issue just before lunch and had to march with our kit bags crammed full with civilian clothes, extra boots and battle dress with usual other kit, back to the billets two miles away. I was leading file walking on the inside. On my right shoulder was perched my kit bag, full to over-flowing, and in my right hand dangled a pair of boots I could not get into it. Firstly, my cap placed of the ap-proved regulation angle fell off. Naturally, being a soldier marching in the town, I could not stop, so the whole squad trod on it to the last file, the corporal in charge picking it up when they had finished. In the course of the march, it found its way back on my head when we had been halted for a rest.

Quick march was soon called again and we were on the second mile of the journey when, turning a corner, I felt the string to which my boots were attached, slip-ping through my fingers. The horror of dropping these ran through my mind and the sudden shock made me hesitate and drop the kitbag instead! Down I bent to pick it up in a sort of hugging manner and by the time I had got it off the ground I was about ten files back in the squad, the men having to break their lines to get round me.

A mixed lot of fellows make up my squad. All ages; from twenty, a postman, to forty, a soldier of the last war; a clerk and a six-foot three inches driver; and all professions from schoolmaster to a carpenter. We all muck in together in the true democratic manner so that often the varsity man is seen out with the carpenter, and a telephone linesman with a stock exchange man. Nobody asks about the other's past life or is much interested in his home town; a queer but rather wonderful thing.

Our billet is another old mill - though very much smaller than Westfield, which is company headquarters. We sleep in a sort of loft - iron beds round the walls, a table and fire in the centre. The fire is lighted at six in the evenings; the smoke goes out through a tall chimney in the roof and gives almost no heat to the room until 'lights out' which is at 10.30. We rise at six and have had our breakfast two miles away long before light.

<u>Back at the billets</u>

Ran out of paper in the canteen. Drill proper starts on Tuesday. The first few days are occupied with the supply of clothes, filling up of endless forms, medical inspection, interviews with C.O., lectures, etc. Our instructor seems to be a good chap. We haven't seen his worst side yet though. His last squad was the best since the one George[*] was in at Whitby and there have been over 200 since then. He is an Enniskillen Dragoon guard. In fact, all instructors here are regulars carefully chosen as the course is so short and so much has to be taught in the time. Between 5,000 and 6,000 men are in this Battalion alone. The expansion is so quick that after training here they can't cope with them all at Huddersfield and are sending them to trade schools in Portsmouth, Grimsby, Glasgow, Reading, etc, so that I may not go where George is after all. Only another month will tell.

<u>Sunday</u>

This morning we had the interview for future trade. I asked for wireless operator as you know and I was placed on the list. The small educational test must have been passed alright, for the officer interviewing persuaded me to have my name put down for O.T.C.B. for training for commission. Of course, he had my past Taunton (school) experience, Certificate 'A' etc. I said I was not keen and wanted to be an operator and he assured me that I would go to be taught wireless and when I was called upon for the interview in three or four months for a commission, I could still get out of it if I wished – so I suppose there is no harm done.

Regarding your money, darling, and before I forget, I have reported that your address has been changed and that the post office is different. You will have to write to the Strand Post Office, Waverley Road, Southsea naming the post office to which you want to apply for your money, so that they (the Southsea one) can send papers on to it. You will be receiving from the Regimental Pay Office, Reading, the book of forms that will be changed for money each week.

I have sent a wire[†] to George to meet me in Dewsbury today at three. It's two miles away for me and ten for him. No train runs direct from Huddersfield and this seemed by far the best way to meet. I would, sweet precious, like your company up here in the evening but I can see that it would not have worked too well. The town is bigger than we thought - about the size of Fareham - but once we get into our working stride there doesn't seem very much time for pleasure except Sundays and at the most an hour a night. It seems now that we will not be here - some of us at any rate - for more than three weeks. Two squads were formed together on Friday last and many men will go to their training battalions leaving only one squad of men to pass out on the square in five weeks.

The men are now lining up for dinner and the two mile walk to Westfield Mill. I will get this posted now and write a few lines when I get back from seeing George. God bless you my dearest. Those three days holiday in Glastonbury were beautiful. May we soon be together again. Perhaps three weeks will see us together. All my love, Roy *Roy's brother †telegram

Tuesday 26th November 1940

Dearest Heart,

Tomorrow should bring a letter from you. You do not know with what delicious anticipation I look forward to having it actually in my hand. An envelope written by you and the contents guided by your own sweet mind is something I could never tire of.

This evening, I had to attend foot surgery with a blistered and sore foot. The orderly told me to report sick tomorrow. I've so set my mind on getting the Blue Ribbon for best recruit that I feel I can't afford the time from training; just my blasted luck! There are fellows in the squad who say they would like a few days rest and it's just like the devil's luck that the man who doesn't want to go sick will be forced to.

Today we had our first *TAB and for the next 48 hours we are confined to light duties. Friday sees our full training start, so perhaps my foot will be alright by then and I will not have missed much.

I met George on Sunday as arranged. Found him looking fit and happy. He sends his love to you. We met in Dewsbury, a larger town than this, 3 miles towards Huddersfield. We met at three, went for a walk along the river, had tea in a snack bar and spent a couple of hours in the music room of a pub. We were the first to arrive just after 7pm, but by the time we left it was full of laughing, joking people let loose by the good beer and excellent pianist. George wanted me to visit Huddersfield next Sunday but a pass is impossible until a fortnight's service. We will meet next Sunday in Dewsbury instead. He insisted on paying for the tea and shipped twenty Players† into my hand on leaving.

The food here is good - amazingly so for men with previous army experience. We dine in a huge warehouse about 50 yards by 80 yards, sitting on forms at scrubbed deal tables. Bread and condiments are already placed on them when you arrive for a meal. A line of mess-room orderlies helps you to food as you arrive at the door and you carry the two courses, one in each hand, to the tables, eating with a knife, fork and spoon carried in a trouser pocket. Breakfast includes porridge or corn flakes, tea, toast and marmalade, with bacon, potato, sausage and fried bread. Lunch is meat, potato and always

Squad 282 D Company Ossett November 1940 Roy back row far right

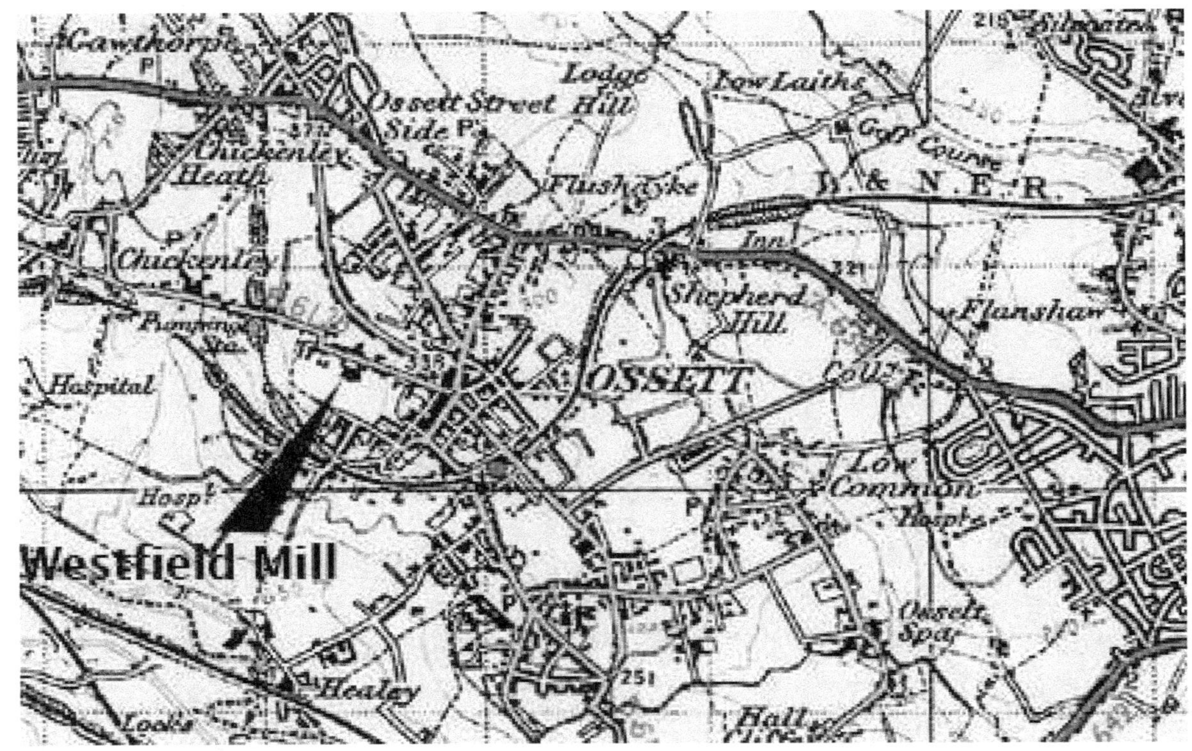
Cawthorpe
Lodge
Low Laiths
Ossett Street Hill
Side P.
Chickenley
Heath
Flushdyke
L. & N. E. R.
Chickenley
Inn
Shepherd
Hill
Flanshaw
Pumpery
Spa.
Hospital
OSSETT
Court
Hosp.
Low
Common
Hosp.
Healey
Ossett
Spa.
251
Hall
Westfield Mill

another vegetable; for sweet always two things together such as steamed pudding and custard, stewed fruit and rice. Tea includes three slices of bread and butter with one pint of tea and a cake, pie or cheese. Supper - soup or cocoa and bread.

Am writing this in bed before lights out. Room is so large and high that the fire makes not a scrap of difference. We have a wireless set but it doesn't work, which is just as well and quieter. All my love, darling, Roy

*Typhoid and Paratyphoid A and B vaccine injection
† cigarettes

Wednesday 27th November 1940

Dearest Wife,

Your letter was given out to me after lunch today. I was several yards away and seemed to sense or see your writing as soon as the letter was uppermost. I could not do anything until I had read your letter twice.

Thank you, for your concern - I am really quite warm. This battledress is very warm; I have not put on vests yet but use the army pullover. We sleep on iron beds with straw pillows and mattresses. I don't need my pullover as the four blankets supplied are heavy and warm. I still have to write to thank your Dad for his hospitality. It's not easy to write in billets and odd moments of the day other than by pencil. I'm told that the Liberal Club, which is open to troops, has a writing room and that paper is supplied to members. I will look in tomorrow and get a letter off.

The foot is a bit easier today and I am wearing the other pair of boots. I missed tea and supper yesterday so that I could rest it, and this morning on account of our rest day we had no parade until 11 o'clock. The whole billet in consequence missed breakfast and stayed abed until 10.15. It was a welcome lie-in after our dark 6am risings.

When the battalion moved from Whitby a few months ago, they took over several mills that had not been used for years. Ossett seemed to be in the centre of the wool and clothing trades; years of depression on account of the fall in exports had made the district a depressed area, and now the government orders for clothing and troop occupation has caused a bit of a boom. Another company 'D' was added to the battalion and although a company normally has 250 men, we have between 2,000 and 3,000 at Westfield Mill.

The people are very hospitable and kind. Most of the fellows have been asked to meals by various families and the men in pubs love to offer you drinks. I met a man today who has offered me a bath each week of my stay and supper afterwards with his family - with my boots

THE LIBERAL CLUB, STATION ROAD

and blouse off and all! 'Got slippers and gown just about fit you,' were his very words.
All my love, darling, Roy

Thursday 28th November 1940
Dearest,

Your letters certainly do brighten up the day! We all seem to sleep warm in this billet - which is fortunate, for many men complain of cold at night and beastly draught. An orderly comes round after black-out to open every window. With windows on both sides of the room it is possible for a strong wind to blow from end to end of it.

I sleep near the door in this room with my feet a couple of yards from the fire. On my left, sleeps a postman and towards my right a wine merchant whose bed is at right angles to mine. A small boy comes in with papers at 7.15 when we return from breakfast. Never once have I had to buy one as half a dozen men seem to buy them from habit and discard them within ten minutes, until this morning when I was forced to report sick and see the doctor. I have to wear gym shoes until Monday, have my foot dressed twice a day and only do light duties. Don't feel pain unless I have boots on - it is the thick boot uppers that cause the trouble - it is so hard and stiff.

Having two ex-soldiers in this squad I am not senior soldier as George was, but stand a good chance of the Blue Ribbon. If you want to get on in this army you have to make a lot of noise with your feet and mouth. Can't do much of the latter but I will work thrice as hard with the feet - when I can put my boots on! Fondest love, Roy

Saturday 30th November 1940

Darling Heart,

We were up at 5.00 this morning to the mess room for fatigues. Twelve men from our squad had to wash up all the breakfast plates. Dressed in suitable clothes and with clogs on we stood at the large sinks, about 3ft by 6ft, from 8am to just before twelve. You can imagine the number we must have done – fortunately, all squads have to do this only once during their stay here. Besides the washing of the plates, all tables and forms have to be washed after breakfast and lunch. We got off at 2pm and another twelve men came on. They will work until ten - washing plates, tables and forms after tea and supper.

Although we had the larger part of the washing at the first part of the day it is by all considered the better fatigue: for we can have as much to eat as we like at the day's best breaks. For breakfast I had 6 large rashers, tinned tomatoes, potato, and two plates of porridge; for lunch, a great pile of roast beef, six roast potatoes, parsnips, prunes and custard; fifteen prune stones decorated my plate by the time I had finished the sweet. It seems that we get such good food because they have the Royal Signals School of Cookery as well as the normal kitchen staff.

Don't know about Army leave for Xmas yet, and of course if I'm moved before Xmas I don't know where I'll be.

I'm going for my bath and supper Monday night as the pyjamas and vest will be just what I want. Laundry day is on Tuesday - five articles being sent free of charge, three handkerchiefs making up one. I've had both my left boots seen to by a small boot maker at the top of this road. Tomorrow, I see the doctor again and will probably be able to wear boots on Monday and re-sume foot drill. He undid the stitching at the back letting a little out. He would accept no payment. Awfully decent these North Country people are. In the bus going to Dewsbury on Sunday I held out 6^d for the fare but the conductor refused to accept payment.

On Thursday and Friday when we were able to stay in bed until 10 o'clock, a little woman living over the way sent in tea, bread and dripping. She wouldn't at first accept any money, but after argument took a penny each for the tea and thick slice of bread with dripping. To see the good sort, you wouldn't think she had a penny to her name.

To give you a better idea of our billets, imagine the mill as a red bricked affair with a large sliding door in the centre. This is never pulled open. We enter through one of those little doors often put in panels of warehouse gates. Stepping through this, you find a cob-bled runway with a loading platform towards the back of the building. Mounting some little steps to the left of this platform the top, about 4 feet above the ground, is reached with our room entered by a sliding door to the left and a long narrow cobbled room used as a wash-house to the right. Above this is the other room somewhat larger than our room, though only taking up half the building in height. Our room goes height of the building, i.e., that of both the washhouse and the upper room so that you can imagine how difficult it must be to heat.

This mill is situated on the northern outskirts of Ossett in a small street with cottages on either side and in front. At the top of the road are three small lock-up shops; the boot mender before mentioned, a sweet shop and a fried fish shop much used by us all. It is kept by two jolly women. One with a husband serving and the other with a son. They do a good little supper for 3^d - chips and a fish cake.

Sunday Morning

The foot treatment I have had has not been successful. I now sit before a welcome coal fire with my foot in a saline bath. This has to be done twice a day for three days more when I hope to be able to start work properly. Five chaps had sore and blistered feet in our squad at the beginning of the week but now I'm the only one left - and my name will be on the light duties list until Thursday at least. I take part in all instructions and duties except foot drill. The heel of my foot was originally blistered. I thought I could fight it off but instead the ankle began to swell until it looked and felt strained and twisted.

The Signals, when they came here, took over for the sick bay, a shop with private house attached. The shop serves as waiting room and MO's surgery; the house above and towards the side as sickbay for the smaller surgical and medical cases. Most rooms being fitted up as wards. The doctor is a charming Irishman, Millard by name. Marvellous personality but hopeless on the platform.

All army doctors must give a lecture to men when they join the army and, like so many people, the doctor is ill at ease when he has to speak from the platform. He passed a moment ago from one ward to another and wanted to know if I was writing to my good lady or taking down the sermon in shorthand. The wireless was on!

Rifles were supplied to us yesterday and I left the

fellows hard at work on them. It takes a good hour to get them into good spick and span order. I did mine last night after the break in this letter - at news time. We have a wireless working now. I think I told you that ours was broken when we arrived. Our wireless expert could not repair it without expense, so two of the men went to the shop, after passing round the hat, to buy some flex so that we could take a lead from the set upstairs. They came back with another set instead! Another example of residents' generosity.

<u>After Work</u> We have the German news on now and they claim to have extensively bombed Southampton again last night, seventy fires burning after a five-hour raid. I had a letter last Friday from Mother with a letter from Uncle Harry inside. All are well at home and I was told to send you Mother's love. Uncle Harry wrote to say that they were well but that during the large raid on Portsmouth last Monday, bombs had fallen outside Plummers, outside the town hall and at Highfield.

Well, sweet precious, I am now off to see George. We are meeting at Dewsbury - can't get a pass for Huddersfield yet. I wish it was you I was going to meet. It would be like heaven to take you into the country, to have tea in some little place and end up in a quiet pub over some chips and beer.   All my love, Roy

Monday 2nd December 1940

My Dearest,

You really are a swell love; this lunch time I received both your Wednesday and Thursday letters and both contained stamps. Now, let me pay my own stamps. The pleasure of writing is worth at least $2^{1/2d}$ to me, and I don't see why you should have to pay 5^d when you write to me.

The food is good but as you suggest few men seem to get enough of it. The *NAAFI canteen at West-field Mill will prove that. They have a large place there and after any meal you will find scores of men drinking tea and munching pies and cakes. I manage beautifully after breakfast and lunch, but in the evenings develop quite a useful appetite which for a few coppers is put to sleep for the night.

I was going to start this while my foot was being soaked but the nurse gave me the paper to read. It has been much better today, I am pleased to say. I was easily able to do gym and even did a little marching with one gym shoe and an old slipper on. The latter has been most useful; tied on with string, which is hidden by a long trouser leg, it is the only thing I can get over the bandage.

George sends his love. We spent much the same sort of afternoon as last week except that we had one of the YMCA North Country Home teas. Meat, pickles, cakes, scones, jam, bread, butter and tea - all for 6^d!

We had a gas lecture this afternoon from 2 to 4. The drills are gradually getting harder. We all feel very stiff after this morning's gym. All my love, Roy

NAAFI Navy Army and Air Force Institutions provided mobile shops for those on active service.

Tuesday 3rd December 1940

Dearest,

One day I don't want to get a commission because I won't have the 6 months with you while training as an operator, and the next I want that commission because of you, the fact that it will take me out of the rut of

Army Life and give me something more than a number. Last night, when I saw the officers and their ladies coming in late and taking the ringside seats at the boxing, I said to myself, 'That is where Phyl should be; not back here at the edge of the crowd amongst a herd of soldiers who can't call their girls their own.' To be an officer would give you a social position that is your right.

Darling, I want, nay must, do something worthwhile for your sake. In all the years I've known you, I feel I have done so little for you. You've been patient, sweet, and kind; so helpful and sympathetic that sometimes I feel less than the dust under your feet, not wholly worthy of your care and trust. For two years you have worked to keep our little home going. You've done it happily and willingly, I know, but why should you have to go out to work - why should you be bossed about in an office, having to keep set hours? No, it's not right.

No, I haven't got a tin opener, sweet. A parcel for the weekend would be lovely - couldn't you get your childhood friend Professor Marzipan to wave his stick so that you could get inside as well? You would be much more lovely and a million times more welcome! Unless you already have the socks, precious, please don't worry to send any as I have 3 supplied and two I brought. I would like, though, either a couple of pairs of my thinner ones in the suitcase, or a couple of pairs of your old stockings to wear under the regulation ones - ladies silk stockings with the tops cut off have been used by several men to protect their feet in their boots with great success.

Jolly good idea about the stove being bought by Budd. Is there anything else we could sell? I will send you a photo as soon as I can get to Dewsbury on a Saturday afternoon. Ossett has no photographer and is a complete one-eyed place. Very poor shops, only one modern front; one small town picture palace; and a theatre-cum-dancehall in the town hall where the boxing was held last night.

I wish I could have taken you to the Fireman's Ball the other night – or stayed at home in the firelight with you on my knee. No matter what task I may be doing, it always seems to be deadened with the thought of our cottage, books and the end of this war. It is the goal I'm striving for and I can think of little else. My love to Jasmine, Dad and to yourself. Roy

Wednesday 4th December 1940

Dearest Wife,

All my thanks for your letters of Monday. No, I am not feeling the cold. You would be surprised at the warmth of our battledress. Nobody wears overcoats yet, not even at 6 o'clock in the morning. I wear no extra

Palladium Picture Palace, Ossett

clothing except my vest; blouse, pullover and shirt are all thick in themselves and a fine protection against the cold.

All but 14 of the squad will leave here the week after next. I don't know if this will include operators or not, but I do know from George that several squads pass out from Huddersfield this month which will make room for some more men from here. The septic part of my foot has now cleared up. I saw the MO again this morning and he is most pleased with it. I'm excused boots until Saturday when I see him again. I'm having my bath and supper with the local family tonight as I couldn't go before on account of my foot.

The kind Yorkshire man who asked me to bring a friend along as well, seemed quite an ordinary little fellow by his manner and dress, but it turns out that he is a partner in a mill. I called at his house last night to make arrangements for tonight and found his home very nice and well furnished, new and modern. Well, darling, I have an hour of clearing up before going out.

All my love. Your own, Roy

Friday 6th December 1940
Sweetheart,

Thank you for the lovely parcel, note enclosed and letter of Tuesday. You are such a sweet darling to make up the nice selection. The scarf was most useful this afternoon when a cold gale sprang up, and I will use it constantly now. It was just like you to buy me one.

This evening I am going to have tuck-in with Marmite as a drink as well as the Ryvita. I sucked those two sweets all the afternoon. How sweet of Dad to put in the cigarettes and socks. Please thank him, precious. I will write to him in a day or two. Again, thanks for the good food and your sweetness. Socks, scarf, cigs and food are the things a service man likes more than anything. I love you so - I wish I could hug you for them. Your own, Roy

Saturday 7th December 1940

My Dearest Phyl,

You asked in your letter yesterday something about my rifle and bad finger which I broke with a cricket ball in my school days. It made me realise that there is still a lot about my life that I still have to relate. As regards my finger - well I cannot of course use it for firing or for the regulation movement of the safety catch. I just use my thumb for the one and the second finger for the other. It doesn't seem to make any difference to one's skill but the instructor wanted to know what I was supposed to be doing at first.

One of the most important things in barrack-room life is the brightness of the laying out of kit. Every cleanable thing must be polished daily and laid out in regulation order on the bed. At the head, the kit bag filled with clothes and personal possessions; on the top, two towels neatly folded and above these and resting against the wall, the tin hat. The straw mattress is folded with the four blankets laid in front of the kitbag; the blankets uppermost. The greatcoat, so folded that three pairs of buttons are showing, stands on the blankets and leans against the kit bag; in front lies the bandolier - only given to mounted units - and inside the circle, a mess tin and water bottle strapped together. In front of this again, standing on the bed springs and against the straw mattress, is a haversack with mug, knife, fork, spoon, gym shoes and extra boots in neat array. To finish the effect the rifle lies at the side of the displayed kit.

You can well imagine the work the equipment gives each day; rifle - half an hour, bandolier - ten minutes, 16 buttons on greatcoat ten minutes and so on; and how annoying it is to have to take anything out of one's kit bag because all the other possessions are bound to fall out of place. Our boots, cap badge and small buttons have to be done before the morning and afternoon parades every day (remember how John used to do his every Thursday for pay parade?) as well as the brass on our gaiters and gas mask case. Gaiters and rifle sling have to be blancoed every night and blankets shaken every other morning in the open air.

The daily work is divided up into four periods - foot drill, physical training, weapons training and lectures. The first parade is at eight o'clock and we march to lunch at 12.30 having had a break from 10am to 10.30. The squad commander was away on leave last week, which gave us rather a slacker time than usual as the corporal, who took his place, was not very strict. I fear our sergeant will be disappointed when he resumes work on Monday, for I don't think we have got any smarter – though we have learnt quite a lot.

Did I tell you that 'D' Company officers and our squad sergeant come from the Enniskillen Dragoon Guards? The second in command of the company and also the Major were Foot Guards, so you can imagine how thickly they lay-on army 'bullshit' (words used by officers and men to describe a particular rule and work expected of men in a unit). We, for instance, have to clean said buttons, boots, etc, before every parade; we get no late passes for after 10.15 at night, neither are we allowed a day pass for another town but Dewsbury for the first three weeks. That is Signals' 'bullshit' because other training units might not be so strict.

If you were to visit us now darling, you would find us a lot of sick men. Yesterday we had the second T.A.B. inoculation and this morning not one of us can lift his left arm above the shoulder. I can't even lift mine on the table to write this. All were in bed last night by 8.15 in both rooms of this billet. It was my turn to turn out lights, remove blackout and open windows and not one man felt like anything but sleep. We are supposed to be confined to billets for 48 hours. We stayed in bed until 10.30, but while last time I didn't have food from lunch from one day to the next, this time I was able to have a cup of hot Marmite, Ryvita and cake last night and this morning.

Your parcel could not have come at a more opportune time, precious. We keep one another in fits of laughter today on account of our stiff and swollen arms. No bod could properly dress himself, had even to wash with one hand; and a few minutes ago, two fellows had to put in an electric light bulb both using their fit right arm. The dose this time was supposed to be 65% while last time we only had the other 35%.

I'm sorry, precious, that you did not get a letter on Dec 4th - you should have done for I have written each day except for Saturday and Sunday which goes to make up one letter. Perhaps it arrived the next day. Thank you for yours of the 4th.

The foot is much better. I hope to get a clean bill of health from the MO tomorrow and resume boots on Monday. On Thursday and Friday, I was given work down at the company quartermaster stores so that I could rest my foot. Had a nice coal fire and a wireless playing while I stamped out identification discs. I was the envy of our whole squad as a terrible gale was blowing the whole two days and nights. The strongest gale I've experienced for many a day.

It was just like you, dear, to suggest sending Mother some eggs. Let's go shares if they can be sent safely through the post. Huddersfield, by the way, has not been bombed yet. Too many a better target within miles. We had a very pleasant time last Wednesday. I took along Joe Byron, a married man from Bournemouth, who is also going to be a wireless operator. After the bath, we had supper of sandwiches, scones, cakes and coffee round the fire. We have been asked to tea on Sunday - tomorrow - and along for a bath and supper at the end of the week. The Langleys are a charming couple and really go out of their way to entertain you.

<u>Sunday</u>

Having read through what I wrote yesterday makes me wonder if you are able to read it at all! My arm is better today. I can at least write on the table instead of on my lap. I put on my boots this morning for the first time in ten days. I should have gone to see the MO but felt too bothered to get up at eight o'clock to sign on the sick parade list. It was the last opportunity to lie in after 6am and I did feel that I wanted to make the most of it. Could you blame me?

Sick parade is a damned farce in the army, for a truly sick man would be dead by the time he saw the MO. Only once a day are you able to apply to see the doctor - that is at 8 o'clock in the morning - when you have to report at Company Office and have your name entered on the sick list. Having had the particulars taken, you have to wait outside in the cold until 8.45 at which time you are marched to the MO's office a mile away. The first time I went sick - only the doctor can excuse you wearing boots - it was a terrible cold morning and the surgery was so crowded that I didn't see the MO until after twelve.

It may seem curious that I have not mentioned any other squad companions by name. The fact is that I have not picked out any particular ones as friends, and although being friendly with all, am intimate with none. I quickly became friendly with two of the men in my room, but when I found them the drinking sort I decided to keep somewhat apart.

I have only been into one pub in Ossett since I have been here - apart from the last two Sundays with George in Dewsbury. Really, not much to do here. Not like our *South Parade Pier and the Sunday afternoon band concerts with singers like Peter Dawson. Now, in my spare time, I drop into the Reading Room of the Liberal Club. They have a nice coal fire there, the papers and plenty of periodicals. Well, precious, I'm just off to tea with the Langleys.

With fondest love, Roy

*Southsea

Monday 9th December 1940

Darling Wife,

Well, I started full training this morning. The bad foot is most comfortable and I felt quite pleased drilling this morning and afternoon. I missed gym as I was down to see the dentist for 10.30. Had one tooth stopped. Some poor fellow had as many as six teeth out at the one sitting; three or four stopped. The Dental Corps Depot here has four different surgeries in the one house and I was lucky to get one of the nicest dentists. He chatted all the time and told me all about his family and practice in Liverpool. Except for having to call him 'sir' I was treated as a private client.

Jack Byron and I had a very nice time at the Langley's yesterday. We spent the time playing Monopoly, chatting and eating. You don't know what a blessing it is to sit in an easy chair and gaze into a coal fire after a few days of this life. We even got to calling them Corrie and Arthur. We both have an invitation for bath and supper, Friday.

Thank you, sweet, for your letter written in bed on the 5th. Don't you dare send me any stamps! You won't have to dream nasty dreams much longer, precious, if my companionship in bed will keep them away.

It will be only a little longer now, dearest. I'm looking to be sent to Gloucester or Edinburgh if it has to be a civilian school. Don't those towns appeal to you, sweet? I got an Observer yesterday and it made me so homesick. Looking up from it suddenly, I expected to see you sitting opposite.
With all my love, Roy

Tuesday 10th December 1940
Dearest,

Just the shortest note as the post is due in a few minutes. We went in the gas chamber this afternoon. Had to go in with our masks on and take them off before we came out so as to get a whiff - stung neck and eyes most painfully and made us cough. Made one realise what a terrible thing gas is - and this was only a mild one.

Another high spot today was that I had two lunches. Had one of hot pot, potatoes, swedes and apple tart which didn't satisfy, so I just walked round in the other door and had roast beef, parsnips, mash and jam tart! I suppose it must have been done before, but no man in this squad had thought of it. Good night, sweet love. I long to see you so.

Your own, Roy

Wednesday 11th December 1940

Dearest,

We will have been here three weeks tomorrow and so enter on the last two weeks of training. Real work has started - our new billets are nearer Westfield Mill and right opposite the home of our instructor. We are the third senior squad in the Company and have fourteen days of blood, spit and polish to passing out day. Not only will we be more supervised, but we will have weapon drill and lectures every night, but Saturday and Sunday, between 5.30 and 7.30pm. All cleaning will be done at night after that hour so that spare time will be very precious. Starting tonight, I will write your letters in the evening and post the next day.

Our new quarters consist of a stable and coach house with loft above; the stable acts as washhouse, the loft as our bedroom. We enter this by an outside steep stepladder. The room is long and narrow with rafters and beds along each side. I say beds, but our old iron ones are no more; for the new ones consist of three planks of wood held six inches off the floor by small wood cross-pieces. Six windows run down one side of the room, the door being in the middle of the wall at the end beside a small coke fire.

My bed is in the far corner away from both the doors and windows beside an ancient piano; the best position in the room. I didn't tell you, darling, that I will actually pass off the square on Xmas Eve and will not be sent away before. The idea of the move was so as to knock two squads into one for the pass-off, the rest of the fellows going to civilian schools before that date.

It is a pity I won't be able to get a living-out pass before Xmas, but all the potential officers must pass out properly. Some fellows will be starting at a trade school next week and they stand little chance of leave. We have one old soldier left in the squad, two home guards, 5 men of OTCs and four potential officers. Competition for the blue ribbon will be frightfully keen.

As regards the commission dearest, I will just let things take their course. It will not come to a head until I have done some training as a wireless operator - for I will refuse a commission in the infantry if it should be offered. You will be joining me after Xmas and that is all I can think of at the present. I think I will have to do the training for operator which will take to next June and then do four months training as Signals Officer! That will take one nearly up to next Xmas.

With all my love, your own, Roy

Thursday 12th December 1940

Dearest,

I long for the day when we will be together again. The days are so crammed with drill, lectures and inter-views that they soon fly by; but just the sight of you in the evenings would be all the difference. I wish you were here in Ossett.

You will be tickled pink and interested to learn that the tea at breakfast is heavily doped with bromide to still the sexual passions of the men! This is a fact and is

openly discussed by the men themselves. The male sex is fond of discussing sex when thrown together as we are, and it was quite brazenly admitted by my squad during the rest this morning that not one had wanted a woman since they had been here. To a woman such discussions must seem filthy, but men thrown together away from wives and lovers are filthily inclined, I'm beginning to think. Darling, I think of you all the time. You are never far away and I love you beyond all other.
Devotedly, Roy

Friday 13th December 1940
Sweetheart,

You are a precious. An unexpected parcel arrived today in your writing and I was able to enjoy a supper of hot baked beans (warmed on the stove up here) and pies. Thank you for your sweetness.

Tomorrow I am booked for bath and supper at the Langleys' but on Saturday I will have the fish and rolls for supper – thanks to you. In the afternoon, I'm going to Dewsbury to have my photo taken and to buy one or two small Xmas gifts for the family. So, don't worry about any of my folk. I thought a photo would do for Uncle and Aunt, Esme and Hugh, some small gift for those at Southsea with another photo. I'm getting half a dozen of these - others being for you and Dod[*]. You said no presents for your family but the children, but I will also give Dad and Jasmine something as well as the photo. As for you, well, I have something in mind for you.

We had weapon drill up here in this room until after eight tonight. I think we will be able to put up a good show on Xmas Eve for our pass-off. All the men are, except one, of medium height - between 5'7'' and 6'

tall. I have been chosen as first man in the front row, to set pace, etc. Although our bed is little more than sleeping on the floor, I slept very warm and comfortably last night. I sleep on my back against the piano leg - a poor position for you darling, but a comfortable one all the same. Good night and God bless you, Roy
Phyl's sister

Tuesday 17th December 1940

Darling Heart,

I came back from my guard duty at 10.30 yesterday morning and there on my bed were three letters from you. Three – and I had hoped for two; but three were a lovely surprise. Three! And I had not even posted your birthday present. I made a special trip to Dewsbury on Friday to have my photo taken and buy you a little birthday gift. We were so rushed on Saturday that I could not get it away, but I hope that by the time you open this, it

Roy's telegram for Phyl's birthday

will have arrived. I'll wait until you join me and we can discuss the pros and cons of a commission. Afraid I haven't seen George the last two weekends to discuss it with him.

I have already bought some cigarettes and a couple of ladies hankies to send to Gresham House with a photo for Xmas. Nothing much this time but it will save you bothering. Just like you to suggest sending something. I have a persistent ache for the sight of you, sweet wife. You are always in my thoughts.
Devotedly, Roy

Wednesday 18th December 1940
Precious Love,

We had our 20 rounds on the range this morning. 'D' Company range is at the top of a hill in a disused quarry; a good vantage point to see the surrounding country. And what a lovely country it is - or was. The firing range is about a mile north of Ossett and we arrived (army fashion) about an hour before time, in this case 08.30.   It was not properly light; the valleys were in darkness and the tips of the nearby hills stood out clearly against a vivid red sky, which had scurrying across its face, puffs of this white cloud. As we stood there, the light gradually filled those wide valleys and the moving clouds seemed to brush the red from the sky leaving it the palest blue. The very sight of it made me gasp. It seemed uncanny.

As the darkness went, green rolling downs fully showed themselves. The grass seemed to possess an unusual greenness; but studded across its face at distant intervals were dozens of tall chimney stacks. Each stack had clustered at its feet the jumbled buildings of a mill; and each mill had this vivid grass separating it from its neighbour, as if each wanted no intercourse with the other, only requiring peace in its own little bit of hill.

These mills stretched as far as the eye could see in every direction and apart from rising smoke, all looked at sleep in a peculiar mixture of rural and industrial life. Incidentally, I was third best shot in the squad.
All my love, Roy

Thursday 19th December 1940
My Precious Darling,

The thought of seeing you very soon now fills my

every thought. It was four weeks ago that I left you on Wells station and I miss you more than I did then. As every day goes by the agony of parting gets more severe. I live in the future - the very near future now, thank goodness – when we will be together again – even if it is a hired fireside and bed.

No orders for this squad have yet been issued about Xmas Eve and we move on to our new station on Friday – that we know, but leave between those two days is still uncertain. I'll let you know precious, at the first moment. All my love, your own, Roy

Sunday 22nd December 1940

Precious Love,

Please excuse shortest note today. Yesterday was spent drilling - except for a short visit to Dewsbury to shop and collect photos. Today has been spent moving to another and better billet opposite the old, vacated by a squad 'passed out' last week. We scrubbed floors, washed walls and windows this morning, moved and cleared kit this afternoon. After the inspection and drilling on Tuesday, the Colonel drives up to our quarters to view laid out kit and inspect room, etc.

This room is much better than the one over the way. It is much cosier, not so high and narrow; a bigger stove, better wireless and piano. These reasons though were not cause of the move. It is a far better room for Colonel's inspection. Tomorrow, we have a kit and drill inspection by Company Commander - hence attention to equipment today. The pass-off is at 9 o'clock on Tuesday and we will be getting up at 4am so as to get kit laid down. I spent an hour after lunch ironing knife-edges to gym vest, shorts, overalls, towel and shirt ready to be laid down for inspection. We drew lots for beds. Instead of a piano at my back, I'm lucky enough to have the stove next to my face - just two feet away!

By the time you get this you will have got a wire from me about Xmas leave. Thanks, precious, for three letters by special Sunday post this morning. I love them - such a comfort. All my devotion, Roy

Christmas Eve 1940

Dearest Phyl,

Another three letters from you today and 30/-. No mention of the *P.O. being my Xmas present but I am considering it as such. The money is most welcome and thank you, darling heart. Your letters coming together represented a joyful half hour at this point of a sad and bleak Xmas away from you. We heard this afternoon that our move would be on Thursday instead of Friday. Apart from the staff, I don't know of anybody getting leave but I held out hopes until the last. I couldn't send the wire until after tea and I feel you won't get it until after break-fast tomorrow. I had so hoped for that leave - in fact, I thought more about it than my work.

A few hours of your company – nay minutes – would be the best gift possible this Xmastide. Only do I partly live without you and five weeks without the sight of you has made the days as like a succession of years. All I ask of life is your company and I am now forced to live a miserable existence dressed in the King's uniform.

Thank goodness the first and worst part of my training is over. Huddersfield brings the rather hateful schoolroom closer again, but it means we shall be once again sharing every free moment I can get. Think of it! It's almost here! You and me and our own fireside! I must make enquiries about a living-out pass as soon as I arrive and look round for some comfortable quarters for you. I've longed for the day of your arrival - it is almost here!

Well, our training, pass-off and inspection are all over - and satisfactorily too. Not a moment did I have to write you yesterday. Drill occupied the day; cleaning and pressing kit - the evening until 12 o'clock (we had a light extension). We were up at 4am to lay out equipment, etc, and prepare ourselves for the morning's ordeal - which, as is usual, was not as bad as we thought it would be.

The Colonel and a senior Major viewed our display after having inspected us. The worst part was the individual salute. Each man in turn - I first - had, after foot drill in slow and quick time and weapon drill, to march 30 paces saluting to the right on the march, to come to a halt in front of an officer, salute, step forward one pace, deliver a message, step back, salute again and retire. As soon as the display was over, we marched back to the billet to stand by our beds, with kit arranged, to await the Colonel who came along in his car.

The best Xmas gift the Colonel could give was bestowed on me. All the time I was working for the Blue Ribbon. I felt I was earning it for you, precious. It is the first step in the right direction, and the blue and white colours will decorate each shoulder for five months. I must run now dearest, as I'm going to a Xmas party with the lads. I hope you have a good time tomorrow. I'll be thinking of you all day.

Devotedly, Roy

Postal Order of money

OS 45,
1st Company,
3rd OTB,
Royal Signals,
Huddersfield, Yorkshire

Friday 27th December 1940
Dearest,

Arrived last evening, same company as George! Eat in same hall, classrooms in same house, billets (private empty houses) about 200 yards apart. Lovely district. High up, nice park country a few minutes. Splendid views of the Pennine Range which is within walking distance for our Sunday outings. You will like it here, I feel sure. Hope to let you know about a living-out pass tomorrow. Only three of the old squad with this one. Nice crowd of fellows. Eight school masters, 1 BBC, Lloyds Broker, 2 accountants, club secretary, 2 lawyers, 1 architect, 2 store managers, 3 clerks, - 21 in all. Started work this afternoon on the Morse Code. Spent an hour with George last night. Treated me to supper at the YMCA. Excuse short note. With all my love.
Your own, Roy

Saturday 28th December 1940
Dearest Love,

Today, my long-awaited interview with the Colonel regarding a commission came to pass. I had expected to see the Ossett colonel but for some reason or other it was postponed to the day of my departure. After taking school and after school particulars, he asked, noting blue and white ribbon I was wearing, if I would like to be sent to an infantry O.T.U. next month - how hard up they must be for officers!

'No, Sir,' I said, 'I've set my heart on a commission in the Signals. Failing that, could I be transferred to an Ordinance Corps with a view to getting one there?' No, a transfer was not possible at this stage of the war with the spring so close. As regards a commission in the Signals, my standard of education was horribly low, for my knowledge of higher maths and electricity was almost completely nil. Would I be prepared to attend a night school for four evenings a week, so as to attain the standard of an examination paper passed across to me?

Well, the questions in it were really difficult – especially on top of all the mysteries of the Morse code, wireless procedures and so on, to learn.

The long and the short of it was that I said I would prefer to think it over for a month, so that I would be able to see if I could tackle wireless sufficiently easily to leave me free to work on electricity and higher maths at night. He was quite agreeable to see me again in a few weeks and making a note of the date, dismissed me.

Candidly, precious, the subject needs careful consideration and discussion. When you come up, we can go into it and by then we can see how my wireless training progresses. George reckons that <u>at least</u> an hour should be spent each night writing up and memorizing notes. That's a bright outlook in itself when we have so many things we can enjoy together in our evenings. Those sweet precious evenings that mean so much to us.

<u>Sunday after Church Parade</u>

I'm afraid you have not received a newsy letter from me since last Friday - Xmas Eve and the joy of the pass-out. For that day, Xmas Day and Boxing Day, we were allowed to stay out until 23.59 hours, a minute to midnight, and you remember that my Xmas Eve letter was concluded with some mention of a party to which I was just off.

A real Xmas party it was, given by a family of nine sisters - all quite presentable too as regards looks - the old mother and father with eight of us soldiers and various family and friends. We played games and sang, before eating a real Xmas supper of jelly, trifle, cake and crackers; with port, sherry, beer and coffee, and turkey, tongue, and beef sandwiches. We were catered for most royally; the real snag was that it made me think too much of you and the jolly gatherings for eight years past under your father's roof. I wanted your presence above everything and there you were spending exactly the same sort of evening 300 miles away. It was hard, my sweet; beastly hard and I don't suppose you were out of my mind all evening.

After supper we played further games and sang until 3 o'clock! It was Xmas Day and the next day was our last day in Ossett, and with a drink inside us we didn't mind if we were found returning at 3.30am. Actually, it was quite alright; for the black-out party that goes the rounds to see if all are in and to see that windows are open at 10.30 each night, came at the usual time and no one was the wiser as to who returned after midnight extension. We had a corporal sleeping in the billet and it was easy to pass him and go up the stairs in stockinged feet.

We had a church parade on Xmas morning after a late - 8 o'clock breakfast. The Colonel led the march to church and read the lesson. Xmas lunch was amazingly good. We entered the mess to find apples and nuts on the table with a pint bottle of beer for each man. I had a most liberal portion of turkey - wing and nice part of the breast - beautifully cooked with sprouts and baked (3) potatoes, Christmas pudding, mince pie and custard. A meal that literally filled me up to the top shirt button and washed down by 3 pints of beer - surprising the number that don't drink here. The Colonel drank our health and we drank his and cheered him. We smoked at the table afterwards and chatted for a solid hour while the sergeants, who had served our dinner, ran round with more apples and nuts.

The real snag about army meals is the rush. They are bolted, and up you have to go to march back to billets. Actually, I have lost weight since being in the army; in fact, nobody seems to put on weight in Ossett. Breakfast and lunch were always ample, but the weak point was the 19 hours between lunch and the next day's breakfast, when nothing cooked was supplied and bread and butter was improved with jam, cheese, cake or meat paste. It's too early to tell you about the meals here, as you can't really judge in three days.

We are billeted in a large house, with hot water after 5pm. Five share my room which is devoid of all furniture. We write on the floor or standing at the mantle-piece, which fortunately is fairly broad. I'm the only blue ribbon in the house and expect something or other that has to be done every minute that I am in the place. Senior soldier is a mixed blessing as he as to back up the N.C.O.s and see that jobs are carried out.

We were at church parade again this morning. One hundred of the Company's two hundred has to go every Sunday so that you have to attend every other week. We muster on the Company parade ground at 8.30; dismissal being about 10.15. I've already worked it out that I will attend without having had breakfast and you can have it ready for me at 10.30. on my return. The other Sunday, we will make up for such an early rising by staying in bed until lunch!

Before I write my application for sleeping-out pass, I have to find a place to live so that address can be stated. It must be within 400 yards of the Company Office. I'm paying a few calls once this is concluded and if I find a suitable place, I will give Sergeant Ford my application tomorrow to be passed on to the CO. So, I should get it through by the end of the week, which means that you could travel up early next week. Think of it! Together, after seven long and weary weeks, darling. I'm so longing for the sight of you. No happier man could be living. The moment of meeting on Huddersfield station between 6 and 8 o'clock one evening next week is all I'm concentrating on. With all my love, precious, Roy

St Patrick's Hall Huddersfield

Monday 30th December 1940

Dearest,

We started work properly this morning and the first instructor was Corporal George Barton who went off the deep end as we did not know all the Morse code. 'You knew you were going to be operators and nobody worried to learn the code at Ossett? You had it given you last Friday, when you arrived, set out on a sheet of paper, and after 2 days you still all don't know it.' I'm afraid my brother made a rather bad impression on the squad and the remarks passed were a great embarrassment to me. His attitude was appreciated by no member of the class!

I had my first duty here last night; Fire Squad member at St Patrick's Hall. The work consisted of sitting at the back of the Hall while a very pleasant concert was being performed, waiting for the spectators to depart at the finish before we left ourselves. Men are called up for the duties alphabetically and in this instance the Bs in our squad were most lucky, for the others have most horrible piquet and guard duties for the next four or five days. Duties that mean either leaving the Company and classroom for the day or sleeping in a guard room.

I'm sure, precious, you will like Huddersfield - particularly this district with nice roads and houses. The town is a 1^{d} ride away or 12 minutes' walk. The shopping centre there is compact and consequently busy. The station, general post office, baths, library, best and cheapest stores are all near together. A large covered-in market and the cheap chain shops, which all seem to be there, seem to attract the most people.

I haven't been able to find any place for you yet. My wanderings yesterday afternoon were fruitless, but

George tells me the other squad passes out from this company this week and, as a part of the men live out, there will be several 'tried' places going. He is going to see the men for me. I can only think of your arrival here. My sweet love, I don't think you know how much I need you.   All my devotion, Roy

On the back of the envelope Roy had written '100 Trinity Street, Mrs East.'

Thursday 2nd January 1941

My Darling Phyl,

Yesterday evening we had another move of billets – the third since our arrival here. A house, empty for about 10 years and about 12 minutes away from the mess room. Foolishly, some of us had the bright idea of carrying our kit along on a canvas bed - coffin and pall bearers wise. Naturally, we were the last to arrive at the new abode and had the worst place to sleep. Right up in the eves, with paper coming off the walls and rotten woodwork, were the only two rooms left. A water tank runs all night outside the door and half a gale blows through it.

You can imagine the comfort of sleeping on the floor! It's impossible to stay up there in this sort of weather, and we are all applying for a shift. January 1st brought in the winter proper. Snow was on the ground first thing and it has been coming down for the last 36 hours. We were supplied with thick vests this morning; up to now no vests have been issued.

I can't believe you will be up on Sunday! The thought of seeing you so soon catches my breath and gives me that sweet pain you know so well. Up to now, I haven't found a place for us both. I should be able to find something by Sunday and have my pass accepted. Will meet any train you mention. Afraid I'm really too excited to think properly. It was only a few minutes ago I heard the news. Am making enquiries about cheap rate for serviceman's wife. Nobody here seems to have heard of it. Darling, simply longing to see you.

Your own Frostie,

Roy

In later letters, we learn that Roy did find accommodation for the two of them at 178 Trinity Street, Huddersfield. Four years later, while stationed in Belgium and writing to Phyl of their plans to live in Bristol post-war, Roy made an uncharacteristically sharp comment on their Trinity Street landlady.

Thursday 22nd February 1945

Dearest,

Many thanks for your letter of the 17th with news of your trip to Bristol and the flat shortage.

Two rooms – I've been as happy as a king with you in one room! Remember the terrible room in Trinity Street, Huddersfield and how the slut of a landlady could be seen in coat and hat, filthy cloth in hand, on pay day?

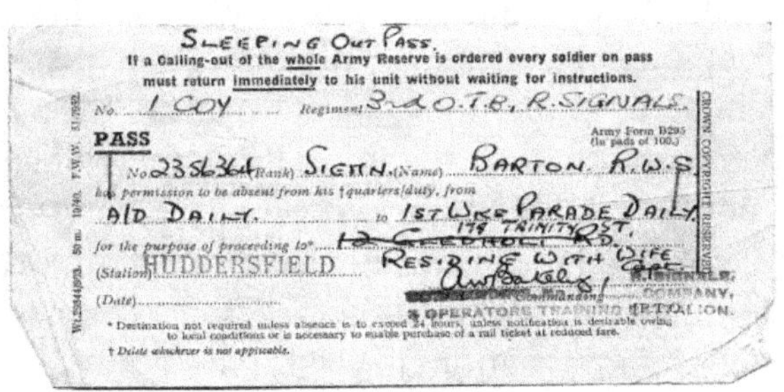

Endnote

In 1988, Roy wrote to me, his nephew, a long document, separate to his letters, detailing his wartime experiences and concluded with these words:

'I had a lucky war. You do not know how lucky. When training to be a wireless operator in Huddersfield, I was given a 'living out' pass, drew army rations and lived in furnished rooms with your Auntie Phyl, who got a job as secretary to the quantity surveyor who was building the ICI dye works on the Leeds Road.'

Indeed Roy 'lived-out' with Phyl for most of his life in the army, until 1944 when he landed with Field Marshall Montgomery's HQ in Normandy. Then, over the next 430 days until October 1945, Roy wrote to Phyl over 200 letters as he travelled through Normandy, Belgium, Holland and into Germany.

Roy was immensely proud of his wartime service in the secretive GHQ Liaison Regiment known as 'Phantom'. Phantom was an information and liaison organisation whose patrols provided a vital communication link between front line troops and Field Marshall Montgomery's HQ to pinpoint the exact locations of the Allied front line and the German positions. This greatly aided Montgomery's strategic planning, not just day by day, but hour by hour. In 1944/5 Roy was the Quartermaster Sergeant in the Phantom Regiment attached to Montgomery's HQ Main of 21st Army Group and because he was out of harm's way, he made time for his letter writing.

After demobilisation in 1945, Roy and Phyl did

settle in Bristol where he worked for a home furnishing business, and Phyl became a secretary at Bristol University working for Professor C.F. Powell, the Nobel prizewinning physicist.

OS45 1st Company 3rd OTB Royal Signals Huddersfield   May 1941   Roy front row far left

Cpl George Barton (centre) and his wireless training section Huddersfield 1941

2756364
A Squad D E d
B Company
2nd S.T.C.
Ossett
Yorks.
<u>Sunday Nov 25</u>

Dearest,

Here sits your husband in the Y.M.C.A. canteen a fully fledged soldier complete complete in battle dress, gaiters & forage cap. The air in here is terrific. Tobacco smoke fills the air, & the noise of voices, pianos, & the clatter of plates makes it almost impossible to concentrate.

To-day we had our issue of kit which just about made me the biggest ass of the British army. We had our issue just before lunch & had to march with our kit bags crammed full with civilian clothes, extra boots & battle dress, with usual other kit, back to the billets two miles away. I was leading file walking on the inside. On my right shoulder was perched my kit bag, full to overflowing, & in my right dangled a pair of boots I could not get into it. Finally my cap, placed at the approved regulation angle fell off. Naturally, being a soldier marching in the town, I could not stop, so the whole squad trod upon it to the last file, the corporal in charge picking it up when they had finished.

'A unique record of service life in World War 2.'
Roy Barton's recently discovered wartime letters include photos and documents from his Basic Training in Yorkshire to his time in Northern France as he travelled with Montgomery's HQ Main through Belgium and into Germany. Roy's 250 love letters to Phyllis also describe the demands of each day, the destruction of German armour at Falaise, the French peasant farmers, Belgian black marketeers, leave in Paris and Brussels, the characters and gossip from his mess as well as their hopes for a 'cottage in the country' and for a baby at the war's end.

ISBN 9781838323905
NOW available on Kindle Books

2356364
Sgt Banton R.W.S.
Adv HQ G.H.Q Liaison Regt
Att' 21 Army Gp. Main
B.L.A.

Friday
19 Jan 45

Dearest,

I have always thought that I would like to write since I was a small child but to me style & sound are such important things that I feel my knowledge is still inadequate. Musical prose, burbling as a brook, is a delight to read for the mind & is also fine for the ears. Three things can move me: music, acting, & lastly, & yet not least, words. In a novel I enjoy the formation & setting out of words as much as the plot & because I do appreciate & enjoy this I realise that I have far to go, & much to read, before pen can be put to paper. I read now but not half enough, & seldom matter good enough. Time will show, darling, but I will probably die unread & unsung — even unwritten! I don't enjoy letter writing & if that can be gone by I don't suppose I would enjoy writing! To my wife gives endless pleasure & is the

Why he had always wanted to be a writer

...tails for hours afterwards. One night was particularly terrible & I will remember as long as I live. The Germans had been trapped & the guns & planes of the allies had wrought terrific havoc & chaos. Tanks & wheeled vehicles lay everywhere smashed & broken, bodies were piled everywhere, paper, food, ammunition & scrap were left not a square yard of ground uncovered for field after field. Every tree & hedge had been blasted of every living leaf & small branch. It was a ghastly sight — far more un-nerving than all the ruined towns & non-existant villages I have seen in northern France.

I see Roy Thomas has been evacuated to England. Can't say what has happened but it need not be very serious as they will only keep a man in hospital for 48 hours before they send him home. One man has been

Roy describes the aftermath of the Battle of Falaise 1944

2356362
Sgt Barton R.W.S.
Rov HQ GHQ Liaison Regt
Att: Main HQ 21 A-Gp.
B.L.A.

Wednesday.
7 Mar 45.

Dearest,

To be actually in the room where Rossini composed "William Tell" ought to inspire one to write something beautiful. Within these walls he lived & worked & so gained immortal fame.

To-day a rather humble British soldier of World War II after a fourteen hour journey from the British sector writes to his wife in England. After eight months away with the liberating Armies he ought to be eager to start his three day leave in Paris. That is not exactly the case.

As long as I live I hope I will never have to stay at a hotel without you. It depresses me. The whole atmosphere of a hotel without your sweet company leaves me more empty than outside these comfortable walls. The fact that some of Rossini's music grew on this spot only makes me want to cry out for you the more.

My very soul cries out for you

Letter from Roy's leave in Paris March 1945

If you have enjoyed
this book,
please consider
writing a review on
Amazon Kindle

www.ingramcontent.com/pod-product-compliance
Lightning Source LLC
Chambersburg PA
CBHW051721050726
47598CB00003B/1000